The Simple Woodcarving B

Simple Techniques for Relief Carving, Easy Step-by-Step Beginner Friendly Projects and Patterns with Photographs

By

Clayton M. Rines

Acknowledgments

This book could not have been written without the guidance and generosity of everyone I have come in contact with one way or another. Your influences are all over this book. Thank you.

Dedication

This book is dedicated to everyone seeking knowledge out there.

Disclaimer

All the information contained in this book is purely for educational activities only. The writer does not assert the accuracy or wholesomeness of any info gotten from this book. The views contained within the pages of this material are those of the author in its entirety. The author/writer will not be held accountable or liable for any missing information, omissions or errors, damages, injuries, or any losses that may occur from the use of information gotten from this book.

Bonus Book

Thanks for buying this amazing book. To appreciate your unending support, we are giving you a great book on Pour Painting that will bring to the forth your painter's instinct. You will derive unending hours of pleasure from practicing the beginner techniques you will learn from this book. Look out for invaluable periodic bonuses in your mailbox.

Download the book by clicking or typing the link below;

https://bit.ly/2LwTK4Q

Cheers

Clayton M. Rines

Contents

Introduction

That thought that goes on continuously in your head as you grapple with how to go about embracing and setting your skills alight with your new-found art love an become an obsession if you don't get the right avenue to let it all out. The amorphous pictures, words, ideas that would only become life forms once you can begin to give that piece of wood form continue to push wanting out from your head. The stumbling block is the lack of knowledge on how to start.

With the almost infinite number of art types that man has experimented with over the years, it is safe to safe that the art of whittling or wood carving is as old as man himself. Carved objects have adorned places of worship, the kitchen, and furniture and beautified other places of interest.

With your interest in wood carving now taking center stage, I can categorically let you know that you have made the right choice in picking this form of artistic expression. The reasons why, are not farfetched as you don't have to break your bank account to get the necessary toolset needed to start working with. The tools are basic, and the wood material is readily available. With your passion, a few bucks, and workspace, you are set and ready to begin carving your dreams into reality.

With some other art forms, functional workspaces are often required. With wood carving, however, you can gather all you need and begin carving in almost any place you find yourself, from the desk in your bedroom to the bonnet of your car or in the dining area.

There is this serene atmosphere that encompasses the wood carving process. The tools are not machine powered; no buzzing sound of engines or welding is involved. It gives you a warm feeling, and you can fully concentrate on the work at and without unnecessary distractions. The tools most times have wooden handles that your hand will find pleasing holding onto for hours. The primary material that design patterns are carved onto, the wood, is yielding to whatever you want to do with it with relatively little or no resistance. There is a sweet fragrance that fills the air as you gently apply the carving knife to the wood.

With wood carving, there is always something for you to carve; the ideas will always come flooding in. The designs can be in the form of intricate and relatively complex subjects or simple chip cuts without well-defined details. Your finished project can be used for almost anything depending on the form it takes e.g., furniture, kitchenware, artworks, etc. The list is endless, and your hobby can become a side hustle from which you generate a constant flow of income and also make your loved ones happy by your thoughtful carved gifts.

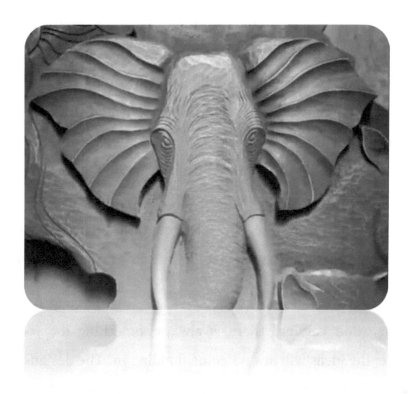

Chapter One

Carving Tools for Everyone

As you start on your journey with wood carving, there is the tendency that you will come across a plethora of tools, and this would most likely put you at a loss on how to proceed. The tools you need as a beginner and tools required to have in your toolkit for the long run are choices that you will need to make. Though there are a few tools that are always present in this wood carving art, there is one that everyone must have at any point in time; that is the bench knife, which is the foundation and spirit of carving.

The Bench Knife

The knife comes with a slender blade with a length of between three-quarters of an inch to about four inches with a gently tapering towards the top of the knife. The cutting face of the blade is sharp enough to be used in carving and cutting wood surfaces. A knife with a relatively short blade is most often called the Sloyd knife, and most folks also have different names for the bench knives e.g., whittling knives, detail knives, straight knives, etc. The variation is just in the name as they all have the same basic structure and function.

With your passion for wood carving taking top priority in your life, you will be getting a lot of tools that will make your experience a worthwhile venture. The most crucial tool in the box will be the bench knife. As a beginner or a long time woodcarver, the bench knife is a piece of device that needs to be well scouted before been purchased. You just don't jump at any type of knife; you look out for only the very best when making that addition to your tool kit.

The Straight Chisel

This tool has the topmost part, which can either be angular (Skews) or flat in shape flattened. The chisel is employed in taking out crisp corners or large surface areas or stop cut when carrying out relief cuts. The chisel can also be put into use in cleaning up the surface of a project to leave an attractive and clean work of art. Skews come in a variety of forms ranging from the dog leg skew, which is used for cleaning up hard to reach spots and for undercuts to the spoon bits, bent gouges, fishtails, and backend gouges.

As you become more comfortable and experienced in the art of wood carving, the number and variety of tools in your kit will invariably increase.

The Front and Back Bent Gouge

These sets of equipment are used for forming long deep cuts in areas where there are curves on the project and also for placing details in aspects of the project that can be a bit difficult to get to.

The Straight Gouge

These set of tools are employed in cutting out a wide area of wood from the surface of your project and also for creating curves on the work.

Round Gouges

These are another essential set of tools to have in your tool kit. This tool has horizontal an end that is blunt. The blade comes in various shapes for a multitude of functions. For example, there are blades with are fully rounded for the u-curved gouges, the rounded curve for the c curve gouges, etc. The tapered horizontal end of the blade is sharp enough to be used cut through wood. The taking out of large chunks of wood at any given time is possible when you make use of the gouge in the initial wood curving process.

Designer Knives

In relief carving, there is a diverse set of specialty knives that can be made use of in the carving. The use and shapes of the blades are as varied as the shape in which they come.

The V Gouge Chisel

The tip of the chisel has a "v" shaped end that impacts a relatively deep line into the wood. The shape of the tip also comes in various v shape from the open v shape to the narrow form. This tool is perfect for those excellent details in your work and inputting some forms close to corners and joints in your project.

The Bent Spoon, Back Bent Spoon, Mallet

With your journey in wood carving progressing nicely, and you are enjoying every step of the way, you will invariably begin to look at more professional and designer tools that will enhance and hone your skills. Some of the tools you should be looking at include and not limited to the back bent soon, bent spoon, mallet, etc. The back bent spoon can get to difficult to reach areas such as the linking points in a piece of design and also the bent spoon us used in taking out large chunks of wood from your artwork.

Micro Tools

For your very fine details, the micro tools will come in very handy. The variety of tools found in this box includes and is not limited to depth gauges, scissors, measuring tape, a toothbrush you no longer use, tracing paper, a cloth towel, files, compass, etc.

The Bracing Table

If you intend been serious about the carving lifestyle, the bracing table is a piece of equipment that you won't be able to do without and must be an integral part of your toolset. The bracing table is constructed from pine and plywood in most cases, and it enables you to firmly hold your work in place while working with some other implements.

The forward-facing part of the bracing board hangs down the side of your table. Your work is then fixed into the holding bay of the bracing table. While you work on the project with the chisel or any other tool, the forward-facing part of the bracing table holds the edge of the table, and at the same time, your project stays in place without moving all over the place. After you are through working on a specific part of the project, you can turn it over or move onto another part by changing its position on the bracing board.

In constructing the bracing board, the following supplies will be required; one piece of plywood (eight inches wide and sixteen inches long with a width of about half an inch), three pieces of pine board (eight inches long and two inches wide) and at least sixteen one inch wood screws.

The lower front-facing part of the board, attach a piece of pine board by attaching it with four of the screws. Place the second piece of pine board to the upper back part of the board and screw it in place with another set of four screws. Also, place the third piece of pine board directly next to the second board and screw it firmly into place. The board, at this point, should have taken the form of a letter Z. Your hand orientation will determine the position of the pine boards on the top part of the bracing board; if you are left or right-handed to make it easier for you to use. For left-handed individuals, the third piece of pine board will be placed at the top right-hand corner of the bracing board while for right-handed folks, the third piece of pine board will be on the left.

When screwing in the pine boards to the bracing board, ensure that it is done vertically and not horizontally. This will prevent the board from coming undone when you are working on a piece of a project during constant use.

Patterns Generated by the Tools

For every tool used on the wood during the wood carving process, a unique design is created. To get started, you should familiarize yourself with the type of patterns that will be formed by the tools on sample pieces of wood before you move to use the tools on your project wood. The blade of each tool can also be used in creating very different sets of patterns depending on the angle through which the tool enters into the surface of the wood and how deep you cut into the wood. For example, if you make use of a "c" curve gouge by holding it at a vertical position to the surface of the wood and enter into the wood at a slight indention while carving, you can create fine semi-circles that add beautiful details to your marine life images. On the other hand, if you enter into the wood in a slanting angle, a fine water drop form will be created that goes in smoothly into the wood and comes back out gradually.

The Cramps

This is a piece of bench equipment that is used in firmly fixing the work you are currently engaged in, in the proper position. There are a variety of clamps, for example, the holdfast and bench screw, which are both advanced tools for professionals and not something that a beginner might need at this point. They are both perfect for works with immense dimensions. For beginners, however, a clamp that can conveniently hold wood of thickness of about four to six inches is appropriate.

The Mallet

This is a hammer-like tool that is used to apply force to the necessary tool on some aspects of a project. The mallet is mostly made of wood with about five-inch diameter with reasonable weight to be able to drive the tool in the desired direction.

The Work Bench

This is one of the essential tools that every woodcarver must-have in the workspace. A proper workbench should be made from eleven by two-inch boards with adequate attention paid to the linkages and joints of the board without a steady bench; your works will be an exercise in futility. The corners of the board should be constructed in such a way that it will not be easily worn out by horizontal force applied to it. The ends of the boards should ideally have an extra inch or two over the stand holding the bench to enable you to fix clamps and other tools. In addition to attaching clamps to the bench, there should also be a bench screw fixed to the rear end of the bench to assist in holding projects which need corners, edges, or other pointed areas carved. The ideal height of the bench should be about three feet from the floor to the top of the table.

You wouldn't want your bench wobbling and moving all over the place when you are working on it; therefore, the legs of the bench need to be adequately fixed to the floor by making use of the appropriate devices.

With years of experience, and as your passion deepens, you might elevate the choice of bench you are currently using to ones that are much bigger with more girth and length.

The Strop and Sharpening Stones

The sharpening of the carving tool is an essential process of the carving experience that every individual must be fully knowledgeable about and also put into constant practice.

Your carving tools, no matter the quality and type, can only perform as well as they should when they have a well-sharpened cutting edge. The strop and sharpening stones are, therefore, an essential component of your tool kit.

When it comes to the stones you employ in sharpening your tools, their quite a few that are of top quality on the market e.g., the diamond hones, Japanese wet stones, Arkansas wert stones, etc. I make use of the Washita because I can quickly source for it, and it is quite easy to use, and as a beginner, you wouldn't want a piece of equipment that is complicated or one which wouldn't give you the results that you desire. It comes in various gradients (fine or coarse), depending on how you intend to put it to use. It is best to have both sets of stones available in your workspace and, most notably, the fine stone for adding that cutting bite to your equipment.

Some stones do need some form of lubrication in the form of a fluid (water or oil). Take time to fully understand the requirements on how to make use of the stone. The Ceramic stone, for example, does not need any form of lubrication for you to get the best out of it. They are small and rectangular, and through all the use you put it through, there won't be the formation of any "hole" or depression in the stone. The top sharpening surface of the stone will always maintain its pristine and horizontal nature.

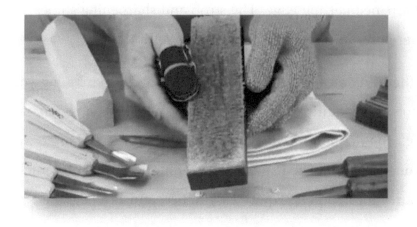

Another type of fine sharpening stone is the "Turkey," which has a fine grain, and if you can't get your hands on the Washita, this will suffice.

The stones come in varying packaging depending on the brand or how a particular set of users want it to be. For beginners, however, you should go for a stone that has no case whatsoever as it allows you to make use of the two sides of the stone. You can make use of one side of the stone for gouges, which brings about a faster wearing out of the stone with deep cut marks and the other side for sharpening fine, flat tools.

If your stone comes without a case and you desire to have one, you can quickly and easily construct one by creating a well-fitted hole in a piece of sturdy wood. A tiny indentation should be made at the end of the space in which the stone will be placed in the wooden block. In the small area, a nail, sturdy piece of wire or screwdriver can be set for when you need to flip the stone over to the other side. Constant lubrication of the stone with the proper lubricant e.g., a 50-50 mixture of paraffin and olive oil, will ensure a seamless sharpening of your tools and longevity of the stone.

Some tools need to have the inner parts sharpened, and this would not be possible with the conventional sharpening stones. This is where the stones with curved sides come in. These stones are called "slips," and the most prominent sharpening tool in this category is the "Arkansas," and it works perfectly on the V tool and the veiner. As with all your wood carving tools, extra care must be taken to ensure that it is well looked after and not allowed to get spoilt in whatever way.

Carving Tools Sharpening Methods

There is no fixed method or style that can be used in the sharpening of carving tools. All you need to do is experiment with different techniques until you get that which you feel works best for you and stick with it. It is essential that once you develop your style of sharpening your tools, you keep to it because once you alter that unique method, a lot of things change, and the most prominent is that angle of the blade.

Your constant sharpening of the tool along a particular path conveys a fixed angle to the blade, and any alteration of these moves will need you to start all over again in other for you to create another angle for the blade to work effectively with.

When you first get your carving tool, it does not come razor sharp. You have to hone it over some time while you use it for your carving projects for it to attain that sharpness you want. There is no rush when it comes to sharpening carving tools; you will have to take your time, carve, and sharp once more until that perfect cutting tool is achieved.

Chapter Two

Your Choice of Wood

The diversity and choice of woods that are used for wood carving depends on the individuals and the project that you have in mind. For the sake of this book and to enable beginners to get a good understanding of woods that will be easy to work on, I will be touching on the woods that are popular for this art.

The woods are classified into two major groups; soft and hardwood.

With the softwoods, you should go for those that you can easily get from the hardware stores around you, and that is easily carved and won't give you a headache e.g., lime, basswood, yellow pine, kauri pine, etc. These examples are excellent choices as they are free of qualities that are of no advantage to the carver or the project that you will be working on.

Hardwoods are the choice of specific categories of some carvers, and examples are Mahogany, Oak, and the Walnut. Looking closely at the oak, the English Oak is the preferred choice as it has a hard quality and a tightly packed grain. The hardwood provides the carver with a rewarding process as the project that comes out of it is full of character and a personality that will stand the test of time. The final touches applied to a piece of hard woodwork are expressed in all its glory if you take your time carving lovingly and pouring all your skills into the whittling of the wood.

When compared to the English oak, the American and Austrian oaks pale in comparison, and most carvers will instead take a wide detour towards the English variety. The grains are not tightly packed with the durable, fibrous material arranged in sequentially patterns to relatively soft tissues. They don't take on finishing touches glamorously as the English oaks. It takes a good eye and a lot of searching before one can get a piece of American or Austrian oak that can be appropriately carved on.

The American Lime (Basswood) is exceptional in the making of wooden toys, turning, and carving. It has a pale yellowish tone, light in weight, and with a soft texture. It is a good candidate for detail works.

Sassafras

This wood has a sweet fragrance and been a hardwood with qualities similar to that of the walnut; it is a candidate for carving and furniture making. It is relatively dense with a yellowish color and dark, tightly packed grains.

The Italian walnut comes quite close to the English oak in carving qualities. It shows the minutest details even better than the English oak, and this is the major reason why it is the go-to choice when ith comes to relief carving. When you are selecting the Italian walnut for your project, look out for the piece of wood that has its grain tightly packed together and quite hard. This is an essential step to be taken as all the pieces of Italian walnut available to you does not mean that they all possess the same level of quality. The dark color of the wood should be devoid of any form of milky white coloration, which is an indication of sap.

The Butternut is a grayish colored wood with an evenly distributed grain. As a beginner, this wood will make a perfect starting material for you.

When the project to be worked on will not entail deep carving, the American walnut will be the wood of choice. This type of wood, due to its nature, does not do well for projects that have fine details because it does not give room for any type of finishing or modeling.

The Mahogany

This wood has a reddish brownish color that continues to darken as it ages. The grain is evenly distributed, it is relatively light in weight but quite sturdy. For your projects that will be entailing the need to incorporate exquisite details, this is your wood of choice.

The Obeche

The Obeche is in the class of softwoods and reacts very quickly to the smallest pressure. Due to this quality, extreme care should be taken when handling it. Your knives should be sharpened for easy whittling of the wood.

Wood types that can be used for carving are numerous, but the availability and the choice of the carver will determine which wood will eventually be used. For this book, I won't be going into details of other types of woods because they are more of the specialty type of woods reserved for select works by professionals and experienced hands.

To carve as is to be treated in this book, the baseline choice of woods is the tightly packed grain oak as our hardwood and the yellow pine for our softwood.

Some woods fall just in between the soft and hardwoods, and examples include the Holly, Beech, and Sycamore. They are perfect for shallow projects with broad shapes, and they are pale in color.

After all the carving has been done on a piece of wood, you should not, for whatever reason, apply any form of polish to it during the finishing process.

An essential piece of information that every carver should always have at the back of their mind is to know that any type of wood that bears fruit or produces any kind of flower will most likely undergo rotting and infestations by worms and other grubs.

Chapter Three

Hand Positions

The angle at which the chips of our project are cut is determined by the fashion in which you place your hand against the wood and the way the carving knife is held. There are some simple ways in which you need to learn to hold your carving knife to form basic cuts on the wood.

To begin, place the carving knife on your hand, the topmost part of the handle should lay in the curve of your pointing finger. The handle of the knife will lay into the holding grasp of your hand. Hold it firmly and gently, with a little pressure yet freely. If you hold it with a bit too much force, the cuts produced will be deeper and more extensive than you intend for it to be, and your hand will get sore and fatigued quickly too.

Cutting the straight wall chips

To make straight wall chips, your carving knife will have to make a ninety-degree angle to the surface of the wood. The middle section where the two sides of the chip meet are to be the part with the most depth. Put your knife at the corner edge where the two linear lines meet before sinking it into the wood.

The Sliding wall chip

This type of chip cut is also found in the straight wall chip. Reduce the angle the blade of the knife makes with the wood. Push the knife into the edge of the straight wall cut and cut the side very lightly.

The Circular edge chips

In the nearest future, you will be working on projects that have curved edges integrated into the design. To make a curve on a project, the angle that the knife makes with the wood is gradually altered as it moves along the drawn line on the wood. The knife is placed at an angle of forty-five degrees to the surface of the wood. Start with this angle and gradually move along the design pattern on the wood then as you approach the middle part of the design, begin to reduce the angle the blade makes with the wood; about a twenty-five-degree angle. Moving onto the other half of the curved design, slowly elevate the blade back to the original angle level you started with. The gradual altering of the angle allows the blade to cut much deeper into the middle part of the design.

The four and three-sided cuts

This type of cut is pretty well used by a lot of beginners as well as experienced hands. Push in the knife at an angle of about forty-five degrees from one side of the triangular pattern. The blade goes into the wood and moves towards the middle of the pattern.

The negative and positive areas

When you make use of your carving knife to chip and cut at the design patterns on your piece of wood, that particular area is referred to as the positive area. The spaces around the cut area that have not undergone any form of chipping or cutting that are untouched are known as the negative area. The design pattern that you are working on can take on any form and shape, depending on the influence you exert on the relationship between the negative and positive areas.

Free-form chip cutting

Rather than the regular chips that are quite popular, the free form type of cutting makes use of a two-sided cut and not the four or three-sided cut. The cut is started at a narrow point and gradually increases as the blade approaches the middle section and then goes back to the former narrow point as it gets to the end of the point. Start with your blade making an angle of about thirty degrees to the wood and increase it to about forty-five degrees towards the middle of the pattern and reduce it as you move away from the center of the design pattern.

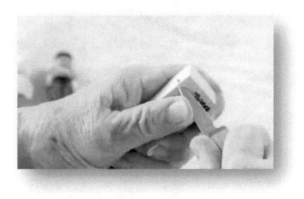

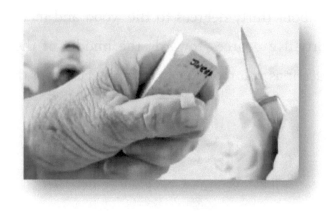

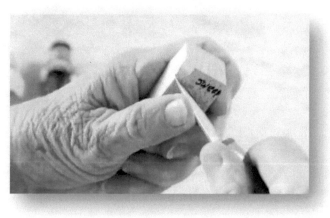

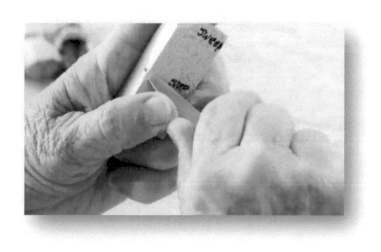

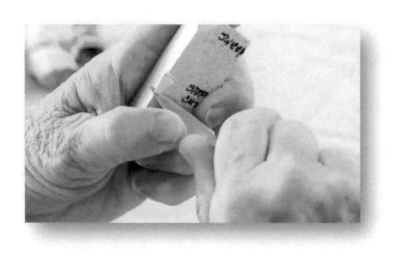

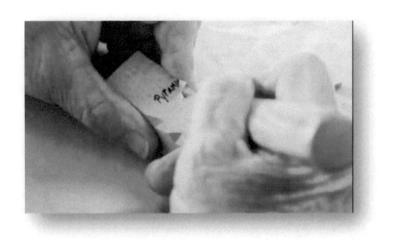

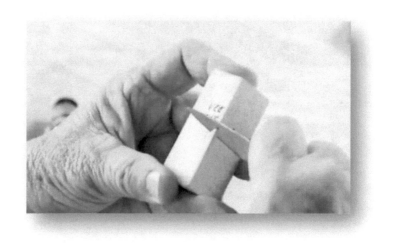

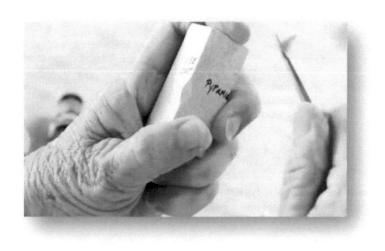

Chapter Four

Producing Patterns

Getting your wood ready

The piece wood that you will be carving is the most crucial part of the whole project as a bad piece of wood won't do justice to your skills, and all the time and effort expended will go to waste. The wood must undergo proper checks and any preparatory touches before you begin the actual cutting. The surface of the wood should be as smooth as possible, free of any obstruction. This makes the copying of the design to the wood surface easier in addition to making the traced outlines visible enough to avoid wrong chips. To get the wood surface ready, employ sandpaper to get rid of bumps, rough areas, speckles of sawdust, and other dirt can be removed using a piece of clean cloth.

The Pattern Tracing Process

Your design pattern can either be hand-drawn or designed on your computer and printed out. The design should fit perfectly onto the area of the wood surface available. Place the paper with the design onto the wood and hold it in place with masking tape or any other tape you have available. Get a piece of transfer paper and gently place it under the paper with the design. The type of transfer paper you use is totally up to you. There is the carbon paper or the graphite paper, which are the common types of transfer papers used.

If you are to use the carbon paper, care should be taken to prevent dark patches from been transferred from the copy paper onto the wood surface. This is brought about as your hand touches a part of the pattern paper during the tracing. Carbon paper gives a sharp image that is cut quickly from the wood without the headache of having unwanted carbon residue on your work. The lines have to be thoroughly cut out from the wood as an eraser cannot be used to get rid of lines that are not part of the design.

A point to note is that if the wood to be carved has a dark tone, a different type of transfer paper will have to be sought for. The dress maker's transfer paper comes to mind as it is available in a multitude of colors and will be visible on the dark wood.

Apply uniform pressure as you trace out the pattern with either pen with colored ink. Do not press too hard and aim to get only the most essential features of the pattern onto the wood as most other finer details are bound to be destroyed when you begin cutting.

After you are through with the copying of the outlines, remove some of the tapes to allow you lift the paper to have a clear look of the wood surface to ensure that you have the exact pattern that you want correctly copied.

The transfer paper is the first and commonly used method of copying designs to the wood surface. The other and an equally as good method is the use of a soft pencil with a lead tip. Using this method, you shade the other side of the pattern paper on which the design you are to copy has already been drawn on. This technique cuts out the need for a carbon paper as the shading already stands in as the transfer agent.

A number 2 lead pencil is used to shade the whole backside of the paper gently. After the shading has been done, turn over the paper and place it on the wood surface. Hold the paper in place with strips of masking tapes. Pick up a colored ink pen and applying even gentle force, trace out the important outlines of the design pattern.

Compared to carbon paper, a soft lead pencil does not leave as dark a line as you will obtain in the former. This makes it easy to get rid of the line as you carve or erase it with the use of an eraser. With this, you can alter the design or introduce new additions as you deem fit. This works very well for beginners as your transfer skills may not be top-notch yet, and you need constant practice to get it right. The soft pencil transfer method will allow you to build your confidence levels with the option of erasing or inputting new details. It is not fixed, and permanent like you will observe in the use of carbon papers.

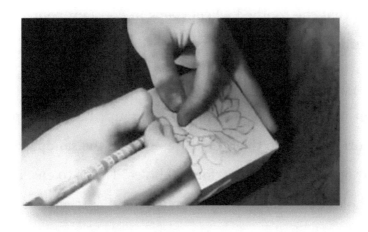

For building your knowledge base and be spoilt for choices on the type of transfer method you want to use, I will touch on one more transfer method.

The pounce pattern comes in handy when you have to carry out more than one trace on the same design pattern. In carrying out a trace using this method, a sewing or pounce wheel is used. The wheels are designed with a tooth that punctures the paper in a uniform designation.

In creating a pounce design, get the design pattern paper ready and a stack of soft old papers. The old papers act as a medium to give easy passage to the wheel when it is moving over the project. Place the pounce wheel over the pattern paper and press down gently and push it along the outline of the pattern. Alternate the direction of the handle of the wheel as you come across straight lines and curves in the pattern to ensure that the toothed wheel keeps in constant contact with the outline of the design.

After you have moved the wheel all over the outline of the design and it is well perforated, picks up the design paper, and turns it over to the other side. Pick up the sandpaper and lightly apply it over the perforated holes. This is to ensure that the holes are thoroughly opened and prevent it from becoming blocked.

After the sanding is done, place the perforated design paper onto the wood and hold it in place with masking tapes. You can then construct or buy a pounce stick; this is a piece of stick that has on one end cotton enclosed in a piece of textile material. It is used in the application of the colored dust to the paper. The pounce stick is dipped into the colored dust; avoid packing on too much dust. Then proceed to pounce it over the trace holes on the design paper. This action brings about a movement of the colored dust into the outlined perforated holes.

So how do you obtain the colored dust? You can get a pack of colored chalks and ground them into a fine powder. Also, the soft lead of a pencil can be sanded into fine powdered form and used as colored dust. There are other ingenious ways of producing colored dust, and you can always come up with one.

The type of colored chalk you use will be dependent on the color of the wood on which you want to work on. For example, if the tone of the wood is dark, bright-colored dust will be preferable to bring about a distinct contrast between the two materials. On the other hand, if the wood is light in color, colored dust like the one obtained from the lead of a pencil will work just fine.

It is not only the contrast and availability of the colored dust that is important when it comes to tracing a pattern on the wood, but the powder should also have desirable sticking qualities. Always carry out a practice run with your colored dust to check if it will stick to the wood surface and even if it will be easily removed when you want to get it off.

After the pouncing has been carried out using the colored dust, remove the masking tapes holding down the paper, and pour the remaining powder on the paper into the storage jar. This is a sustainable way of transferring patterns.

Chapter Five

Design Reduction and Enlargement

Most times, that drawing or design you want to carve out on the wood will not be a perfect fit for the work at hand. This is an almost everyday occurrence as you will not ever almost get a design pattern that will fit right into the project that you have in mind. So how do you go about making the best out of the pattern you have in hand to work best with the project? You either reduce or enlarge the design pattern. To do this, you need to have a picture or image of interest in hand.

Let's take an example of the face of a lion. This carve makes a lovely decorative piece for almost any room in your house and also as a gift. The size of the lion face or head you have in hand needs to be enlarged for it to be of any reasonable artistic value based on the result you have in mind, which is to hang it on a wall. The larger it is, the better it draws attention and is appreciated.

The pattern of the lion head has a dimension of 4" by 6," and the work surface has an area of 8" by 12". The image carving will have to be double the pattern size.

On the design pattern of the lion head, using a pencil and a ruler, create well drawn out boxes that measure half an inch by half an inch.

Go to the bottom left-hand side of the pattern and begin by marking the box there with either a letter or number and progress upwards to the top left corner of the pattern. After you have gotten to the top left corner of the pattern, go back down to the bottom left box and begin marking it with numerals or letters moving horizontally to the last box to the right-hand side on the same line.

Get an everyday piece of paper, and making use of a sharp pencil and ruler, set up a grid measuring one inch by one inch. The new piece of plain paper is the base of the new pattern that you want to create. Mark each of the new boxes just as you did with the old ones.

The reason for marking each box is so that you can have a point of noting which part of the image you are transferring at any given time. Taking on each of the boxes one at a time, create the new lion face image to the enlarged design.

Making a Design Simple

When a design pattern interests you, and you want to carve it out, you will discover that a lot of the time, the picture contains numerous fine details that will prove hard to incorporate into your carving. To overcome this obstacle, you should consider the main features and outlines of the pattern that is to be carved.

In a situation where there is a recurring feature in the pattern to be carved, to simplify the project and at the same time retain the distinguishing features of the work, make use of a contour shade technique to bring all these features into one unit. In aiming to carve multiple elements, one can spend an excessive amount of time and, at the same time, get tired. Lumping the features together makes your carving experience a more enjoyable one. An example of a recurring feature that can be grouped is the feather of a bird.

To give you a simple guide on how to group a recurring feature of a project, start with copying out the major outlines of the pattern that defines and confers a distinguishing feature to the work. There is no point in trying to carve out all the lines in the project as it will eventually be removed as the carving project continues. The lumping of recurring patterns most times, when they are relatively small into substantial features, makes it easy for you to carve out rather than spending endless hours on small individual elements.

In some projects, the features to be carved are unique and not so closely related that it will require grouping. In this scenario, to make the project as simple as possible, apply the levels technique.

The larger areas that have undergone simplification by grouping together of small units are to have a deeper carve area compared to more minor features. On the pattern design, the areas that will be eventually undergoing a deeper level of carving will be shaded darker by using a pencil. In contrast, areas with relatively shallow carving will be lightly shaded.

There might be a need for you to refer by labeling the different parts of the design pattern to guide you as to what each part is when you are working on the project at a future date.

Chapter Six

Levels

When working with a project that has lumped together related items, you will note that all the details were similar; that is, there is a relationship between them e.g., the scales of a fish, the feathers on a bird or the leaves of a tree.

As you progress with your wood carving experience, you will come across projects that do not conform to the example of having similar features. There will be situations in which the number of features you will have to carve are numerous with no close relationship whatsoever. For example, you might start by carving a boy sitting on a fence in a meadow. This provides you with the opportunity of carving a project that has different elements, and all you need to do is try as much as you can to make the project simple.

For any design project that you will be working on, there will be a minimum of three to four layers. There will be the main focus of the project, which is also called the prime object, the background on which the prime object will appear, and other layers to be integrated into the scene of the carving. The number of layers that can be presented in the design is not limited, and you can have as much as six or seven. The number of layers will increase when there is another area of focus other than the primary area in which the prime object appears. To make your project have equilibrium without appearing disjointed, aim to have at most six layers and a minimum of three to four layers. Having too many layers in your work makes it noisy and quite hard for you to keep it neat and straightforward.

For the boy on a fence carving feature, the prime object of the design pattern is the boy sitting on the fence with the rolling meadows serving as the backdrop. The other area of focus is the scattered trees.

Start with marking or lettering the levels from the letter "a" to "f" progressing from the innermost part of the carving, which you should tag "a" to the part nearest to you as "f." It will be of artistic importance if you place and work on the prime object at a position centered right in between the nearest and farthest parts of the carving, which will be ideally tagged "c." The boy will have two levels at his back, and three levels placed ahead of him.

The placement of the prime object at this position is essential in providing shades of contrast to the features present in the carving.

Chapter Seven

Carving Letters

The inclusion of letters, numbers, and other inscriptions add a touch of uniqueness and identity to carved works. Wedding gifts, birthday presents, jewelry boxes, plaques, etc. are perfect examples of carvings on which letters can be carved.

Let us take the project of a frame with the face of a black bear carved into it. There are spaces at the bottom and the top of the frame into which you can input lettering into the project. To get started with getting the perfect lettering and carving, here are some simple steps that you should embrace;

Get a piece of thin transparent paper and draw or write out the letters you want to be transferred to the wood. Set the paper and draw the outline as you will want them to appear on the wood. Then proceed to cut out the letters one at a time. Place each letter into the space you want it to appear on the wood surface.

The arrangement of the cut letters should be appropriately arranged to have even spaces in between them. Fold the piece of paper into two in such a way that it touches the last and first letters. Then fold the middle part of the paper into two halves over the middle part of the design. The lettered design pattern at this stage should be aligned to the face of the bear.

You should note that letters have different spacing requirements. Some letters need ½"; some require ¾" while others do well with 1" spacing.

Try as much as possible to mix up the fonts you put to use. The type of font to be used, however, depends on the kind of project and the letters to be used. The boldness of the words and the font types convey a message. The bold types of fonts covey and action while the not so bold words indicate a person or personality.

How large or rather the height of the letters also conveys a message of importance. The larger the phrase or words, the more it passes across the message that it is intended to. For example, if I carve out the word "Florist," it will be the boldest and the most significant word while other words or phrases will pale out in comparison, having relatively smaller and less bold features.

The orientation of the words also draws attention. Some of the words can be in italics, flowery, or some other formats. Not all the words need to maintain a horizontal and uniform pattern as it can be a bore and not stand out enough to catch the eyes.

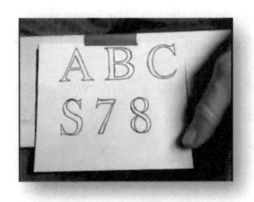

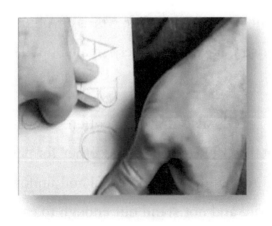

Getting Fonts

There is a multitude of places from which you can get fonts to be used for your project. You might be aware of sources of free fonts, but I will quickly run through it for folks who might be having challenges with this.

The most obvious place to start from is Google and other search engines. Input the phrase, "fonts free download copyright free." You will be presented with several options, click the website that offers you want you need. On your desktop, create a folder named "New Fonts" and store your new downloaded fonts in there. Some of the downloaded fonts will come in zipped files. You will need a software to get the required data out successfully, and this process is called extracting. The WinZip application is the most commonly available and used application for this procedure. When the zipped file is opened, there is the possibility that you will come across several files; look out for those ending in .ttf or .tt. The records obtained from the zipped file are to be saved in the created folder for easy access.

To easily get the wanted files and easy location, follow these simple steps;

Go the desktop > My Computer > Search > Enter into the C drive > windows > click on the folders named Fonts > desktop > highlight and cut .ttf files only > paste into the Fonts folder > delete the New Fonts folder on the desktop.

Chapter Eight

Carving Landscape Relief

Once you get into wood carving, you are guaranteed an almost infinite number of hours of unlimited pure joy. The wood carving starts from a plank of plain wood to a finished piece of artistic brilliance that lights up the room in which it is placed.

In relief carving, the main point of interest is in the alternating and ever-morphing design pattern and textures that you can bring to forth and not necessarily how deep the knife cuts are. Taking the example of a boy sitting on a fence in the meadow, slightly curved cuts are used to show the rolling clouds, long and short thin cuts indicate the grasses, vee-shaped grouped elements show the leaves on a tree while the tree itself is a deep vertical cut. The fence is a series of continuous vertical and horizontal long and short cuts, and the boy is indicated by curved and short vertical cuts in the wood. All the cuts come in different forms and formats, giving varying textures to the work.

As a new convert to the art of carving, relief carving offers you an avenue through which you can hone your skills. There is no essence in you laboring for an eternity carving a multitude of repeating elements to get a work of outstanding features. With relief carving, you will be exposed to the opportunity to develop your carving methods.

The Essential Methods Employed in Relief Carving

Electrical Power Machine Carving

The use of electrical power tools over the years has edged its way into the carving methods that carvers employ in developing new works of art. These portable and handy tools carve through bits that are made of sturdy materials e.g., diamond, steel, titanium, or some other stuff. The prices of the carving bits can be on the high side when compared to the carving knives, but at the same time, the bits are not that expensive that a passionate carver won't be able to afford. The higher the price and quality of the bit, the more the exquisite smoothness of the work it will produce. If you can't break the bank for a high-quality bit, there is the likelihood that an uneven texture will be created, and this can be worked on to give a smoother finish by making use of a sanding paper and other knives and tools.

For folks who are not fans of power carving, making use of the hand-powered tools can make your relief carving a speedy and effortless process as it can be used for roughing while you then apply the finesse and smoothing later on.

The Hand Carving Technique

Making use of this method involves you holding onto the carving knife and other cutting tools and applying sufficient force to make cuts. The tools come in various forms; there are cutting tools that are held in one hand like the cutting knives, and there are others that are held with two hands, with one hand moving the cutting edge in the path you want it to go and the other hand applying force to the tool to move it forward.

Using the Router Method

The tools used in this carving method are best for individuals who have set up a room specifically for wood carving. The router can be altered in such a way that the relief level to be carved into the wood can be adjusted by altering the height of the tool. The bits of the routers are also varied, and they most times give a rough cut, which can be further smoothened by hand carving tools or a relatively smaller cutting bit. By fine-tuning the rough cut, you will be transforming your work into a perfectly carved relief work of art.

The Mallet Way

When the project you have in mind is of considerable size and the wood is not that soft, then your choice of cutting tool should tilt towards the mallet. The tip of the mallet has a horizontal cutting blade with a sturdy body. The cutting blade is held in close contact with the wood of interest, and the thick body is struck with a desired heavy object to apply sufficient force for the blade to move in whatever direction you want it to.

The mallet cutting tools are available in various thicknesses from the relatively light ones to quite heavy types to cut more substantial amounts of woods.

To make use of the tool, the cutting blade is held with a hand and the hitting object, which can be a mallet or some other heavy tool in the other hand. Just before you begin to use the mallet and cutting tool on your piece of wood, ensure that you make use of a workbench on which the piece of wood is correctly held in place to prevent unwanted movements all over the bench.

Relief Carving Levels Treatments

I have been discussing the variety of methods that can be put to use in design patterns before the actual woodwork of carving starts. Another pertinent aspect that you should always have in your checklist is having a mental image and strategy of how you will texture and add finishes to the area surrounding your prime objects. There are quite a few ways through which you can achieve this, and some of these pathways are discussed below.

The Indented Curved Background

Using this type of relief carving technique, leave about 3 inches of space from the outer edges of the wood before you start carving deep into the wood. Gradually start working a slight depression into the main carving spot. Due to this indentation that you have incorporated into the project, it is quite evident that it takes on an integral part of the artwork. Some folks might leave the corners of the design wood with the sharp corners. Still, if you want to bring in the edges into the mix, you can add some of your finishing to it e.g., adding some patterned curves or some other forms of design to point to the fact that you have not left out any part of the wood in this design. A gradual carving in and downwards gives the impression that the work has more depth compared to what it has.

Gentle Inclined Background

This carving treatment is observed in a lot of projects works with a slow and gentle gradient moving from the main carving itself to the boundaries of the design pattern. This method allows for the objects of the relief carving to be the center of attraction.

To put this technique to work, first outline the design you have in mind onto the wood and ensure that it doesn't get to the edges of the wood. Leave about 2 inches of free real estate between the main design and the edge of the wood.

Making use of the appropriate carving tool, cut out the specified area around the main design. Gradually work with a round gouge roughing into the design, cutting, and chipping away, reducing the initial height of the wood around the design pattern. After you must have done this and gone to work on the main design, at any time later, during the project, you can still go back to add some touches to the edges with a chisel to add some finesse or smoothen it out.

Enclosed Boundary Background

Take the example of the boy sitting on a fence, a well designed patterned frame in an enclosed background will be perfect. The boundary can take on any shape from rectangular, circular, or square, depending on your choice.

To start, from the edge of the main design, using a ruler and pencil, measure out the desired distance, which can range from half an inch to one inch. Do this at regular intervals all over the edge of the design and try as much as you can that it is uniform. Then proceed to trace out the line with a light leaded pencil gently. Making use of a gouge, rough out the marked areas before employing a chisel to add finishing touches.

Saw Cutting Relief Patterns

Quite a few relief pattern projects are of the outdoors, with trees, a few buildings here and there, and the main subject. Such carvings most often are worked into woods with a definite shape. There are some relief carvings; however, that is not bounded by these fixed frames and can be carved as close as possible into the very outlines of the design pattern.

There is often time the need to put in place levels in the patterns been created. The levels all have different depths and can be established in the process of the rough out.

For relief carving, the individual design spaces have different height levels on the working material. For the boy sitting on the fence, the image of the boy is the topmost part of the design, the fence and trees are a step below the boy, while other features such as the clouds go deeper into the wood.

The carving can begin by first roughing out the different design patterns into selected levels, which can then be carved out into varying height levels.

To make the carving out process easy for you, mark out the different levels with signs, numbers, or letters. For example, the boy is "a" the fence and trees; "b," clouds "c," other features "d," etc.

Relief Carving Steps

To produce a relief carving project, the work must pass through five simple steps.

The initial steps are termed the roughing out process during which all the levels you have indicated will be in the project will be produced by cutting to a preselected level in the wood.

It is a way of taking out unwanted wood from the areas around the wood to begin showing the unrefined images of the design. To get this done easily and quickly, make use of tools with large cutting blades to get down to the depths you desire without much hassle e.g., the bench knife or any of the wide blade gouges. After this roughing out, the initial impression that you will have is that the work is rather shabby with jutting out of angles, no curves, etc.

When the initial rough cuts have been made, proceed to give definite shape to individual elements in the design pattern. At this stage, some finer details like the rolls, tapering, contours, joining of two distinct areas together in smooth graduation will begin to appear as you take out the sharp jutting remnants of the first step. The perfect tools to use for this step are the skew chisel or the straight chisel, and you might also decide to throw the bull nose chisel into the mix.

You can then move on to shaving or the removal of strands of woods that are remaining. This shaving or smoothing can be done by using the straight chisel, bench knife, wide sweep gouge, or the bull nose chisel. Hold the shaving tool against the surface of the wood, creating a small angle and gently push in small short strokes to create a flawless, smooth surface.

After the shaving must have been completed, it is now time to add more gleam and shine to it by sanding it. When the sanding is done, clean the surface with a piece of clean cloth.

The final stage is the addition of finish to the carved work. This touch brings out the beauty of your work, and it makes it stand the test of time. When it comes down to finishing, a lot of factors are to be considered, such as what the artwork is to be used for and your taste of paint types. There are two main types of paints that give shine and burst of color to your artwork; acrylic paints and craft paints. Other finishing materials include and are not limited to sealers and oil finishers, which prevents the effects of aging from quickly deteriorating the wood while also at the same time increasing its artistic value.

Flawless Backgrounds and Linkage Lines

As an individual who is relatively new to the art of wood carving, you are likely to be confronted with some challenges such as how to create clean and flawless backgrounds and get those joint or linkage lines as perfect as you can. There are quite some methods that you can employ in your wood carving projects that will help you in surmounting those problems. Let us get started.

Carved Curved Areas

These types of areas are quite easy to access, and a bench carving knife can be used to make stop cuts to vertical lines that can belong to the walls of a building, tree, or some other objects. After the stop cuts are in place, proceed to put your knife slightly beneath the surface of the wood at a perpendicular angle. This method will generate chips, and it will generate sharp, faultless edges in your work.

Simple and Free to Reach Joint Angles and Lines

In some projects, you will have linkage areas that you can easily have access to, and the choice of tool you make in creating a stop cut is dependent on the space that needs your attention then. Given this scenario, I will advise you try out some of the tools in your tool kit e.g., the bench knife or v-gouge, and you will finally decide on which to use as the task at hand determines.

Begin by making use of the bench knife or v-gouge in the angle and push in the tool in such a way that an angle is created as it goes into the wood. The depth of the cut should not exceed the length of the tool. This affords you the opportunity of returning to that area to carry out any fine-tuning that you might want to carry out. A gentle approach to easily smooth and work on an angle is preferable to cutting it out aggressively.

After the angle is a bit close to the level you want, start to use a gouge (the large round one) to rough out the space.

Closed- Difficult to Access Linkage or Joint Lines

To get into those hard and seemingly impossible to reach spots, a tiny round gouge or a u-gouge and the carving bench knife will come in handy. Just like you will do in the carved curved areas, make a stop cut on the straight lines. Gently place the bench knife on the wood surface and ever so gently, drag the knife towards you. These prevent the lumping together of the wood strands that can result in uneven cut lines leading to a disfigurement of the work.

When you are through with the first step, move onto placing your knife underneath the wood surface and remove a tiny piece of wood. Sliding your knife under the wood will come to a halt once it gets to the position of the stop cut leading to the piece of wood coming off. This step should be continued until you have attained a depth at which the cuts go below the stop cut you initially made. When you get to a depth below the stop cut, the wood chip won't come out as it did in previous cuts, you will have to construct a new and small stop cut to take out that piece of wood.

When you are through with removing the wood chips to the desired level, smoothen the area with a veining tool.

Chapter Nine

Type of Cuts

The Stop Cut

The stop cut is used in differentiating varying height design types that are present in a work. It involves a bench knife and you making two precise and delicate cuts in the wood.

To make a stop cut, your bench knife should rest on the outline of the design, the blade of the knife should be on the exterior line edges of the design, and then the blade should also make a slight angle with the surface of the wood. Applying a uniform force on the knife, draw it along the line of the pattern, making a gentle cut as you pull it. After you have gotten to a point, stop and remove the knife from the cut then move to the inside of the line pattern, a few distance away from the actual line that you have cut before. The knife should make a slight angle with the surface of the wood and then applying some pressure, draw a well-formed stroke. A trough-shaped in the letter "v" will be formed through this two-step action.

This is how to make stop cuts, and it can be performed repeatedly over the same area to deepen it further and distinguish the level from the surrounding areas.

When the stop cut must have been made with the bench knife, it is then the turn of the round gouges to gently drop the surrounding environment into where the stop cut has been made. With the stop cut, the gouge will not be able to make any cut in areas higher than the stop cut.

The Chisel Push Cut

The varying types of chisels can be made use of when there is a need for the formation of a well defined straight line. The chisel should be firmly held and apply some force into the wood to bring about a clean cut.

The Chisel Back Up-Cut

Align the chisel, the angular part of the blade against the working surface, and push gently to obtain an obstruction-free surface.

The Chisel Back Down-Cut

This method is best applied when there is a rough cut to be made. Place the blade of the chisel on the pattern outline and push the blade deeply into the wood. This will create a cut with a relatively massive depth.

The Round Gouge Cut

This type of gouge is perfect for the removal of large amounts of wood swiftly and creating a well-formed depression on the wood surface. After the initial carving steps, the application of the round gouge is necessary for the creation of levels in the design pattern. The tool comes with a half-pie point that is efficient in the creation of cuts of considerable depths.

The gouges are perfect tools for shaving, too, as you push it harder, the more the tool will go deeper into the wood. With evenly distributed force and ever so light push, you are bound to get wood surfaces that are a beauty to behold.

The V-Gouge Cuts

Instead of making a v cut in two separate cuts with a bench knife, you can get this type of cut in one single move with the v- gouge. The cutting edge od the tool is designed in the shape of the letter v, and there are different angle sizes of the v-gouges available. Some of the v-gouges will give you an angle with open angles, and some of the others are good at making narrow angles.

As with any cut that you make with your carving tool, it is best that you go along with the grain of the wood and not against it. Flowing with the grain of the wood prevents unsightly and deep cuts from been made. The v- cut can be produced by fluid movements of your hand and the tool from a particular area or towards a point as long as the direction of the wood grain is put into consideration at all times.

This tool is not only perfect for the construction of angles, but it can also be used in the smoothening operation of your project works. Align one side of the v point of the tool against the side of the wall and push forward in one smooth move.

Chapter Ten

Irregular Design Patterns

Designs with no regular fixed patterns make for exquisite additions to any wood carving project. They add another dimension of curves and flowing motion across the levels on the wood. The challenge that any carver would face is how to integrate the initial design pattern to the wood surface due to the lack of reference points; most notably the curves through which the identification and marking of the individual areas of the pattern can be performed. As with any challenge, there is always a solution, and with a problem of this nature, you can still work out a way of setting up your unique marking points so that you can quickly transfer the design pattern to the wood.

For this form of addition of a design pattern to a plank of wood, I will be using a rose flower as an example. The petals of the flower are irregular with curves. The rose pattern on a piece of paper when folded into two would encapsulate the main features of the design pattern that you would want to be transferred to the wood. After the initial fold, you can then move a step further and fold over the piece of paper once again. Unfold the paper, and then using a pencil, mark out the significant points on the paper where the curves of the rose petals are. The points are the markers that are moved to the wood surface and allows you to quickly and seamlessly trace out the flower.

The rectangle and square-shaped method have been used in this instance, but other methods can be used, such as the triangular, c- curve, or s-curve method. They are used depending on the shape of the image you want to be transferred to the work surface. Uncomplicated and easily formulated designs bring about ease of copying the patterns to the wood.

Circle Creation

You will inevitably come across design patterns in your wood carving journey that will involve some forms of circle. These forms may not be an integral part of the carving, but they can be part of the fringes or borders of your work. Wherever the position of this spherical or oval design is found in your work, it will always make an excellent addition to the carved project.

Getting the circle pattern traced directly to the wood surface is the easy way out. You can also aim to improve on your freehand drawing skills by tracing the curved lines without tracing it. If your hand drawing game is not top-notch, you will still trace the already prepared circular pattern badly. In essence, practicing and been able to create a freehand drawing of curves and circles will always come in handy for you.

With the boy sitting on the fence, you can add another feature of a rainbow in the background. To do this, locate a point on the design and mark it as the middle point of the rainbow or the circle you are about to draw. At that point, get a pin and insert it in there. To that pin, affix a piece of twine that will go at least three times to and fro from the center of the circle to the edge of the circle. Tie the cord in such a fashion that it will conveniently touch the edge of the pattern and drape it over the pin at the center of the pattern. Get a pencil and put it into the twine, and draw out the pencil to the end of the string. Now draw the circle by moving the pencil along the route the twine makes form the center of the circle.

Chapter Eleven

Safety when Woodcarving

The health and safety of the individual carving and those around cannot be taken for granted at any point during a woodcarving process. The health and steps to ensure an injury-free environment is a primary step any aspiring or experienced woodcarver should understand before a carving project is embarked upon. As you learn the rudiments of woodcarving, safety should also be an integral part of the process of making every woodcarving process a fun one. In as much as the carving of wood can be fun, this will come to an abrupt end once there is an accident. Though accidents might not be prevented, with the use of safety gear and other invaluable tips, the severity of any mishap will be drastically reduced.

Your Health

Quite a number of the woods used in carving have resins and oils that can cause allergic reactions to individuals who are susceptible to them. Woods that fall in this category are mostly tropical in origin. It goes without saying that whenever you are sawing, drilling or making use of any form of machinery on such woods or even any wood products, put on a dust mask that prevents the inhalation of tiny wood particles that might cause severe reactions to the respiratory tracts and other parts of the human body.

Some woods do have spalting on them; the spalt is a form fungus that grows on trees, and it can be extremely harmful to the human respiratory organs. To know if a piece of wood has spalted, you will observe some dark lines streaking across the wood. These lines make for exquisite kitchen arts and other forms of decoration; it is the spores that are toxic and not you touching or working on the wood itself. To prevent coming down with any potential side effects, always ensure that you wear protective equipment during the processing of such woods.

When cutting or making use of power equipment, put on protective goggles to prevent splinters, chips, dust, etc. from getting into the eyes. The use of power equipment and the constant chipping and cutting of wood will fill the room with particulate matter, which will inevitably cause respiratory tract problems. In your workspace, install a vacuum fan that will remove any form of dust generated during the carving process.

During the carving and cutting process, there is a high possibility that some fragments of wood might pierce your hand or some other parts of the body. Since such wood splinters are not clean, there is a high chance that it will be carrying some form of microbes that can bring about infection of that particular area, which will quickly spread to other parts of the body. If you experience an injury from a splinter of wood, promptly take out such material, clean the area of penetration, and, if possible, seek prompt medical attention. The sure way of reducing the chances of getting your hands harmed by the splinters of wood is always to wear a carver's glove. At all times when a carving project is ongoing, you must have the gloves thoroughly worn on both hands. The carver's gloves do not have a fixed left or right-hand design, as they can be altered on each hand at any given time. High-grade carver's gloves have some form of steel thread fabricated into the design of the glove to give it extra protective capabilities. Other glove designs do not have steel thread integrated into the design, and these types of gloves tend to have a firmer grip potential when compared to the steel types that can cause slipping of the carving tools. There is also the leather carving glove that also offers a reasonable form of protection to your hands. The chances of getting any sort of injury to your hands are seriously reduced with the protection provided by wearing the hand gloves.

The carving aprons are made from leather, and they come with a pouch for storing some wood chips and other non-dangerous stuff. The apron should be worn when carrying out any type of wood carving activity as it protects your torso from potential harm.

Let us move on to hand tools and the safety measures you should always put in place. When carving with a sharp bench knife, you are safer than when you employ a blunt knife. The reason why is because the sharp bench knife cuts easily through the piece of wood, and you don't have to apply a lot of force to get a cut made. This cannot be said for a blunt knife that will require a lot of force to get a cut made, and there is the possibility of the knife constantly sliding or jerking off the surface of the wood leading to accidents.

The carving knife should be appropriately held in a firm grip when carving. The handle of the tool should be held in your hand of choice, either right or left, or any of the hands if you are ambidextrous. Holding firmly to the knife will give you a comfortable measure of charge. The thumb on your hand holding the knife should be the guiding force ordering the direction and flow of movement of the carving knife.

When your carving knife or any other carving tool is not in use, they should be placed safely into the tool kit box. This is because the sharp edges can cause harm to the human body and any other materials around the home.

When carving is in session or just before it begins, doesn't it make considerable sense that the piece of wood been worked upon should be fixed and prevented from moving about? It is not only about the aesthetic quality of the work that is produced that will suffer serious defects, but the health of the carver is also at risk. There are quite a few implements that can be used in holding down carving to the workbench e.g., a carver's belt, clamp, vice, etc. Your body parts will be kept away from sharp tools and other power-driven machines.

When power machinery is being used, there is the tendency that a loud continuous stream of noise will be produced. To ensure that you don't suffer any permanent ear damage, put on ear protection guards.

When you are about to turn on your power tool, always make sure that it is at the lowest speed setting. You can then gradually increase the speed as you deem fit.

A rheostat is a must addition to a die grinder with the inclusion of a cutting head. The die machine comes up straight when powered on without almost no form of regulation or control. If there is a faulty cutting head or some of the screws are loose on the cutting die, the die can cause some horrific injuries to the body.

Woods will always have unwanted visitors in the form of insects and other bugs that bore and lay eggs in them. These bugs not only damage the quality of the wood, but they can also be a source of infestation to the home or any new environment that the wood is introduced to. When buying wood for carving, it is advised that you carry out a proper inspection of the wood for any sign of holes made by insects. If you, by chance, failed to spot any bug and take them home, you can use an insecticide to treat the wood.

Get a large plastic bag and place the wood in it alongside a large can of suitable insecticide with the cap off. Secure the top of the plastic bag well to prevent the entrance of air or the escape of the insecticide once sprayed. Depress the top of the can containing the insecticide and let the plastic bag sit in a corner for a few days. When you are ready to retrieve the wood, take it outside the workspace or the home to a place with proper ventilation and to not let your nose get too close to the bag when opening it. To be entirely satisfied that every last bug, larvae or egg has been cleared off, a repeat of the steps is highly needed.

Other Essential Safety Tips

Attention

When cutting the wood, your mind should always be focused on the task at hand. Always try to envision and think several steps ahead of the likely path the cutting tool might take. Be fluid in how you set up your body and don't be fixed or rigid to one particular position that might not be comfortable or likely to cause bodily harm. Be one with your wood carving at all times. Do not let your mind wander while carving as once your mind begins to drift away, you are prone to accidents happening. Make use of your eyes, ears, smell, and all your other senses when carving. Do not be caught unaware at any point in time.

The Pressure

The more pressure you apply to a carving tool, the more the propensity for the sharp blade of the tool to go out of your control and cause harm. This issue of the application of force and accidents is most common with newbies as experienced hands have mastered how to direct and channel the force applied to the carving knives. It is more or less the driving of a car; once you do not have control over the driving force, injuries will most certainly occur. Whatever the type of method or technique you decide to use in your carving process, always weigh the control it allows you to have over the knife, the wood, and your environment at all times. With time and more carving projects under your belt, you will be more proficient at developing equilibrium between the pressure and control you have over the direction of the carving tool.

Your Outer Reach

Before you begin carving, stretch out your arm with the carving tool in hand. The area all around you that the tip of the tool reaches is what is termed the safety zone. It is often a circle around you, and no one should break that circumference whenever you are working. Once an individual comes close, stop any carving at once and put your carving tool away.

The Inner Reach

While you are on the lookout for external interference that might get hurt, you need to also look out for number one; that is you. Always make sure that the blade of the carving tool is at no time pointed directed at you or held in such a way as to cause bodily harm. The best way of ensuring that no accident of this sort ever occurs is to have a clear picture of the potential paths that the blade can take at all times.

Finally

Woodcarving, as an art, can be termed as been dangerous due to the tools involved. Do not shy away from this passion of yours due to the facts I have stated above. All you need to practice is safe and conscious carving at all times.

Chapter Twelve

Woodcarving Sample Projects and Ideas

Taking up wood as a base for artistic projects and other functions serves as a way of taking care of numerous environmental conditions such as the presence of greenhouse gases in the atmosphere and it is a far better option of gift items than plastic and other non-biodegradable materials that harm humans and the environment. Woods are carbon sinks and hold onto excess carbon that would otherwise have caused severe damage.

There is this allure and beauty that comes with wooden artifacts that no other material can provide. The diversity of projects that can be produced with wood is almost infinite. I will be touching on a few basic projects here with step by step guides and also providing you with some wonderful project ideas to develop with the lessons you must have gained from this book. Now let us get going.

A Rose

Supplies

Large round gouge

Bench knife

Straight chisel

A basswood board

V-gouge

Graphite paper

Masking tape

Sandpaper

A pen

Directions

- Place the basswood board on the workbench and hold it firmly in place with the aid of a vice, clamp, or some other securing devices.
- With the aid of appropriate grit sandpaper, smoothen the surface of the wood.
- Draw the rose pattern on a plain sheet of paper or search the internet for an image of the one you like. Place the paper with the design on the wood surface and hold it in place with some a piece of masking tape.
- Get the graphite paper and gently push it beneath the white paper with the design pattern.

- Gently and firmly trace the design pattern on the white paper onto the piece of wood.
- Pick up the bench knife and lay it at an angle of about 80 degrees to 90 degrees to the surface of the wood just a bit outside the outlines of the design pattern. Cut this line.
- After making the first cut, place the bench knife at an angle to the line of the initial cut and produce another series of cut, and this will create a trough-shaped in the form of a v from the outside lines of the design pattern.
- Fix your bench knife at an angle of forty-five degrees into the well-defined corners of the design. Dip in the knife and remove the chip that was formed.
- Now comes the time when you employ the small round gouge to reduce the areas surrounding the design pattern to about one-quarter of an inch. Move along with the direction of the grain and move the gouge from the areas surrounding the rose design towards the direction of the rose flower itself. Remove any strands or sliver of wood making use of the bench knife.
- You can carry out dressing of the outlines of the rose flower at this point with the aid of your bench knife.

- Distinguish the petals, flowers, and other parts of the plant by cutting through the design lines in place with the v-gouge.
- Make the leaves of the flower stand out from the petals with the straight chisel. It is essential that in all the cutting and re-cutting, always flow along with the grain of the wood.
- To distinguish the central part of the flower from the petals, create a stop cut with the v-gouge.
- At the central part of the flower with the petals surrounding it, form a depression using a small round gouge.
- Add finishing touches to the outlines of the flower and peals with the straight chisel. You can then go over all the cuts you made initially with the different tools to make very light touches to smoothen it out. After this must have been done, get a sandpaper of correct grit size, and smoothen out the carving. Remove the dust with a piece of cloth.

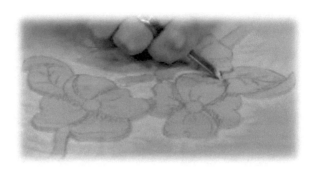

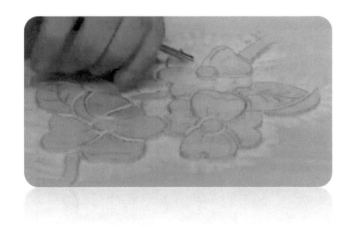

Wooden Spoon

Supplies

Block of wood

Hook knife

Bench/ carving knife

Sandpaper

Hatchet

Directions

- In carving a spoon, a block of wood that has the grain flowing in the same direction will be the best option for you here as it won't give you any challenge during the carving process.

- Set up the block of wood on the workbench and secure it.

- Using the hatchet gently cut out a relatively flat side of the wood. Do not hack away, instead make directed and well-aimed cuts in direction with the grain of the wood.

- A push cut should then be made on the wood (the push cut is a method whereby you hold the block of wood in one hand and using the other hand holding the bench knife, you make cuts flowing away from your body until you have attained the desired level of evenness in the wood.)

- After the wood is even enough for you, pick up a pencil, and make a drawing of a spoon on that flat surface. It doesn't matter how pretty or rough the spoon looks at this stage; all that is needed is the outline to enable you to carve.

- Set up the wood in an upright standing position with the head of the spoon facing upwards and the other parts facing down.

- Start carving along the grain of the wood with the carving knife, taking out chips and bits of wood at the junction where the head and handle of the spoon joins. Be patient and do not rush this stage; take out tiny pieces of wood one step at a time. This is to prevent you from making a mistake that cannot be reversed if you chop out more wood than you should have.

- A point to note here, at no time should you carve the drawing of the spoon directly. Carve just outside the outline of the drawing of the spoon.

- Turn over the slightly carved block of wood with the handle facing upwards and the head downwards. Create push cuts leaving some real estate of wood around the area where the head of the spoon is; about half an inch to one inch of space is ok.

- Now is the time to make use of the hook knife in creating a depression by pressing downwards the part of the hook knife that is not sharp while the sharp blade makes the cut. The first few downward cuts might be a bit hard as you will need to firmly hold down the piece of wood with your free hand while the other hand holding the hook knife works. After you must have gotten a few substantial cuts, the process becomes faster and more relaxed, and the depression in the head of the spoon will begin to take shape.

- After you have gotten the right depth and curvature for the head of the spoon, you can then move on to shaving off the wood remnants on the side of the head of the spoon.
- The next crucial step is resizing the flat side of the spoon. After you must have drawn the flat side and removed any unwanted wood, the unique outline of a spoon will be discernible.
- Now you can move onto the last aspect of the project, which is the sanding. Here you will likely spend a lot of time for the finished work to be as eye-pleasing as possible. The sanding is done in stages with grit paper of three types; the low grit (400 grit) to remove any sharp or rough edges, medium grit (800 grit) for enhancing the unique features of the spoon, then high grit sandpaper (1,200 grit) to make the spoon smooth and attractive.

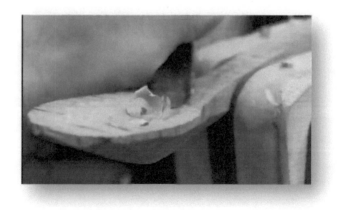

Wooden Tobacco Pipe

Supplies

Wood; 1 ½ inch square by 6 inches

Sandpaper

Drill

Kerf saw

Rasps

Files

¼ inch drill bit

Workbench

Clamp

Natural oil finishing (Olive oil)

Directions

- The initial step that will be undertaken is the drilling of the bowl that will be holding the tobacco. The hole mustn't be too deep because the pipe will be linked to the bowl from the lower part.
- When you begin to drill the hole into the bowl, start from the middle to ensure a uniform distribution of the wood around the holding bay for the tobacco.
- Now you can move onto the boring of the stem of the pipe. The location and arrangement of the stem of the tube are significant. You should try as much as possible

not to bore the stem too close to the bowl. The length and depth of the hole can be ascertained by inputting the drill bit until it touched the end of the tunnel.

- Place the drill bit into the entry way of the stem hole and then proceed to check if the hole is adequately aligned by placing your finger on the outside of the stem.

- The bowl of the pipe will now undergo some shaping. Begin with carving with your bench knife all around the sides of the wood. When you are through with that of the bowl, move on to the carving of the stem.

- With the lines now taking a fixture on the wood, proceed with carving and chipping off any excess wood.

- After the carving is done, round it properly with rasps and sanders and take care not to be too hard to damage the structural integrity of the pipe. You can check if there are any faults with the pipe by sealing the opening of the bowl with your hand and blowing hard into the stem. A well-carved pipe will not allow for the release of air from any part of the wood. If, however, there is an escape of air from any part of the bowl or stem, get some wood glue and apply it to that part. Seal the bowl with your hand again and suck in the air lightly to draw in the glue to seal off the air escape route.

- With the rounding out done, get a sandpaper of the appropriate grit size and sand down the pipe.

- Apply the natural oil finish to both the exterior and inside the bowl. Turn the bowl all around to ensure proper coating of inside the bowl is done.

The Forest Spirit

Supplies

A bench knife

Pencil

A piece of birch wood

Directions

- Start with drawing a face on the wood. The face can be of your favorite movie or cartoon character.

- When carving the wood, take your time to do it patiently because once a piece of wood is carved out, it can't be replaced. Carve it gently.

- Carve out the design pattern of the face drawn onto the wood with the stop cut technique applied to the mouth, eyes, and nose.

- Carving out the eyes is the next logical step. Do it steadily till; some eye shapes may be shallow while some have some depth to it. So carve until you achieve the level you are looking out for.

- Dust the face and add some features with your pencil. Some of the features add expression and personality to the face.

- Remove the top layer of wood that is on the eyebrows and let the under layer of the wood bark stay so that a contrast can be made.

- Carve out the wood at the position of the nose, removing the bark of the wood till you get to the inner portion of the wood.

- Move on to the mouth.

- The forest spirit most times comes with flowing and full beards. So this should be an integral part of the carving projects.
- When you are done with adding the beards and the mustache, use a sandpaper to remove the unwanted sharp edges.
- Dust off it off with a piece of cloth.
- There are a variety of face types, beards, and mustaches that can be carved onto your project. Let your imagination run wild and get creative!

A Wooden Chess Piece

Supplies

A piece of softwood (2 inches by 4 inches)

A bench knife

A large knife

A saw

Sandpaper

Directions

- Begin by drawing out the shape of the bishop, queen, soldier, or pawn. If you have the image in your head and feel you don't need to draw out the figure before carving, you can go straight into the carving.
- The cuts should be a bit rough at this stage, and some pieces of wood need to be left on the carving for fine-tuning the figure later.
- With the figure and features of the chess figure carved out, sand it lightly with a piece of sandpaper.
- You can also add some finishing by rubbing down the chess pieces with a natural oil like olive oil to add some sheen to it.

Wooden Bowl

Supplies

A block of wood

Hatchet

A straight carving knife

Sandpaper

Adze tool (curved)

Measuring tape

Directions

- On the block of wood, draw the features of the bowl.
- Measure how thick you want the bowl to be as this will guide you during the carving and how thick the bowl will eventually turn out.
- The measurement will guide you in creating the perfect outline. Join all the points from the measurement.
- Start to form a depressing in the center of the woodblock with the Adze tool. The cutting path should be in a downward fashion, cutting gently from one side and then moving onto the other side of the woodblock. Carve away at the wood in gentle strokes and do not aim to remove large chunks of wood at a single go. Cutting from the opposing ends of the woodblock allows you to get a uniform depth just like you envisioned it to be.
- As the depth of the depression in the wood becomes more pronounced, you will have to become more accurate and gentle to avoid it becoming too deep as this is not reversible.

- When you have gotten the desired depth, start with the formation of a uniform and even wall on the inner part of the bowl with the straight knife or the Adze tool.

- With the wood held down firmly with a clamp or vice on the workbench, start with taking out excess wood on the outside of the wood. The design pattern you drew will be the guideline here.

- The push cut is the technique to be applied here. Your attention should be fully on the process to ensure that you don't go below the thickness level you have measured out earlier.

- With the outside wall of the bowl done, move onto the sanding. This will remove any unwanted sharp edges or uneven curves. Make use of grits of varying sizes as you aim to smoothen the inside and outside walls of the bowl.

- To make the bowl shine and attractive, combine a mixture of olive oil or beeswax to bring to the fore the artistic attributes of the bowl.

Rose Flower Inspired Wooden Clock

Supplies

Blank basswood (1 inch by 5 inches by 20 inches)

Bench knife

Band saw

Carbon paper

Brash wire brush

Drill bit and drill

Battery clock

Palm sander

¼ inch to 3/8 inch gouges

1/8 inch to 3/8 inch skews

Sable brushes

Compass

Sandpaper of varying grits

Directions

- Get the piece of basswood and prepare it to a length of about twenty inches. If the clock will have curves on the bottom and the top, use your pencil and a measuring tape to mark out that area.
- The wall clock in question will have arches at the top and bottom, so take a measurement of 3" from the top of the wood and mark it out. Move on to the side of the

wood and take another measurement of 3" and mark it out too.

- Pick up the compass and set it to 3".
- The compass should sit at the median line between the pencil line from the top of the wood and the pencil line from the side of the wood.
- Carry out the same process at the lower part of the piece of wood.
- Make use of your saw to cut the arch and sand the edges with a rough, mild, and very fine sandpaper.
- It is now time to design and work on the face of the clock by designing the area where the face will be.
- Go to the middle point of the curved arch at the top of the wood and take a vertical measurement of 3 ½ ".
- Measure 2 ¾" from the side of the wood just below the arch.
- Set your compass to about 2 ½".
- Fix the compass into the middle part of the lines.
- Draw out a circular area that you want the face of the clock to sit.
- Set up the site for the battery.
- Go to the middle point of the lines from the top of the curved arch and the line from the side of the board and create a hole with a drill bit of 3/8".

- The drilling should be done from the front of the wood to the back.
- Get a piece of sandpaper and form a cylindrical shaped mass with it and push it into the hole to remove any slivers and smoothen out the rough drill.
- Set up the outer edges of the face of the clock to about 1".
- Use a pencil to mark out this boundary.
- Go to the back of the wood directly behind the clock face and set up a rectangular area where the machinery of the clock will be located.
- Measure ½" from the top, bottom, and sides of the clock and mark it.
- Measure 2" from the topmost part of the arch.
- In the well line, measure 2 ¾".
- Now measure the clock machinery and remove the measurement from the width of the wood board.
- The number you come up with will serve as how deep you need to carve out from the well in the wood e.g., if the clock has a thickness of 4/8" and the wood has a thickness of 1", the depth of the well will be 4/8".
- Place the paper with the design pattern onto the surface for the wood and the face of the clock too.

- Using a masking tape, hold the piece of paper with the design in place before sliding the carbon paper under it.
- Trace out the flower design with a pencil, remove the paper, and the carbon paper then proceed to carve out the floral pattern.

Wooden Table Lamp

Light is life, and it is a source of joy when it appears in the darkness. A well-carved table lamp is a perfect gift to anyone or a family.

Cloth Peg

Everywhere you look now; you will mostly find only plastic pegs. Wooden pegs are from an era already passed, and you can have a taste of the lifestyle form way back by producing this nice work of art. The pegs can come in various forms to give a hint of diversity and mystery to the pack.

A Wooden Mug

The usages of a well crafted and designed mug can test the boundaries of the imagination of the owner. You can use it for quite a lot of functions e.g., on your desk at the office to store pens, pins, etc. or at home for other purposes.

Jewelry Box

A jewelry box with fancy designs carved onto it is a delight to behold at any time for the owner. Now picture you gifting this box to a loved one, their smile will surely light up a room.

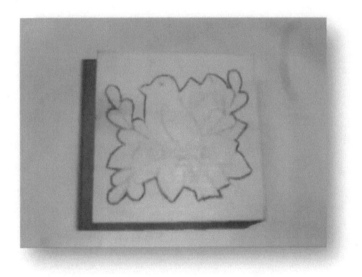

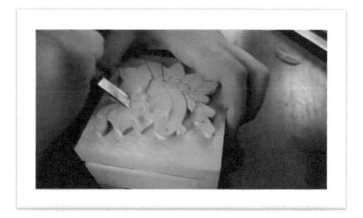

A Picture Frame

A picture is eternal, and it speaks a thousand words. A picture frame with the right images carved into it is a beautiful gift for a birthday, wedding, anniversary, or any other function.

In the End

Woodcarving is life in itself, and the allure and skill set gives a beginner or experienced woodcarver the opening to give bare pieces of wood a new lease on life. It lets your imagination and dreams come to life; your ideas take shape and form in the piece of wood that lies on your workbench. As you begin your woodcarving journey, ensure that you carve responsibly, save the planet by not buying tree products from illegal sources, and always put your safety and those around you into consideration at all times.

Other Books by the Author

The Simple Beginners Guide to Cricut Explore Air 2: A Manual on how to Setup Cricut, Design Space, Cricut Project Ideas, Troubleshooting, and Essential Tips

Are you interested in upping your craft game with the Cricut Explore Air 2 or any of the Cricut brands? You are here, and that is all that matters now. This is the guide that you need in this ever-morphing environment of designs. There is always something new to be learned in the world of Cricut if you are a professional or a newbie. Why hold onto yesterday's ideas that will make your work look outdated? It is time that you take a dive into the amazing world of the Cricut Explore Air 2 and other Cricut brands to learn and relearn some of the following;

- An introduction on what the Cricut machine is
- The different types of Cricut machines
- How to unbox and setup the Cricut Explore Air 2
- Understanding the different types of materials that you can work on with your Cricut machine
- Choosing the material settings
- How to use image files
- Installing and Uninstalling the Cricut Design Space

- Making use of Design Space
- Installing fonts from Design Space
- Uploading your image to Design Space
- The Basic set of the Cricut Tools kit
- Pairing the Cricut Explore machine through Bluetooth to the Computer
- Resetting the Cricut Explore Air 2 Machine
- Using Print and Cut in Cricut Design Space
- Vinyl tricks
- Amazing DIY Project Ideas
- Sample Projects
- Tips that a lot of folks overlook about the Cricut machine
- Maintenance for your Cricut machine
- Troubleshooting
  And so much more!

https://www.amazon.com/dp/1702647226

The Pyrography Beginners Workbook with Exercises

Learn to Burn with Step-by-Step Instructions with Introduction to Basic Tools, Techniques, Modern Wood Burning Textures and Patterns, and Sample Project Ideas

The art of pyrography, also known as pur graphos (fire writing), is as old as mankind, and this form of art gives immeasurable satisfaction to artists by giving power to the imagination. This book opens up a brand new vista to you, laying bare all you require to begin your journey with this timeless art. In The Pyrography Beginners Workbook with Exercises, Clayton M. Rines shows you the basics of writing with fire, types of tips, pens, shading techniques, and other lesser-known methods that help you develop your craft. You would learn the in and outs of buying your first pyrography machine, types of woods to burn, safety tips, maintaining the workroom, and other essential tips for successful wood burning projects. This book offers you some easy to carry out projects as a way of getting you accustomed to the art of wood burning, from making of wall clocks, key holders to creating cup coasters and bangles with images.

You will learn;

- Easy projects for everyone
- Learn how to write, shade and apply outlines
- The importance of temperature settings
- Knowing what type of burning nibs to use
- Important safety tips

- Must know techniques for texturing and finishing
- Burn those great gifts for your loved ones
- And so much more!

With The Pyrography Beginners Workbook with Exercises, you are on your way to becoming a pro in wood burning carvings, wooden plates, household items, and so much more.Grab a copy today and begin your pyrography journey.

https://www.amazon.com/dp/1674755775

A Guide to Wood Finishing for Beginners: A Step-by-Step Manual on How to Finish, Refinish, Restore, Stain, Dye and Care for your Furniture

This is the ultimate wood finishing guide for an exquisite project.

Applying a well-thought-out and researched finish can bring out the beauty and shine in an otherwise bland work. On the flip side, a well-built and alluring piece of woodwork can be turned into an ugly duckling with a lousy finish.

Clayton M. Rines takes you on a journey through one of the aspects of woodworking that many crafters will rather avoid. He removes the cloud of mystery surrounding wood finishing. You will navigate the minefield of finish application, refinishing, and staining with ease like a pro. You will discover new and existing methods that work on how to select the best type of finish for your project, correct errors, prepare the wooden surface, and troubleshoot.

As a beginner or a pro, it is pertinent that you understand the basics of staining, coloring, and dyeing your wood. This will give you a wide array of options to play within any project, thus breaking down restrictions that might have been in place. When you fully understand the foundation of wood finishing, you will be able to bring out the hidden beauty of your wood, promote its longevity, and make the whole wood-crafting process a seamless experience.

"A Guide to Wood Finishing for Beginners" is packed with invaluable tips and hints that will enlighten you on the reasons why you should go through the process of finely finishing your wood, the methods to embrace, and what to avoid.

You will learn the following and much more ;

- Simple and safe method of applying spray finish

- The different types of solvents, oils, and varnish

- The types of wood and how to apply finish to them

- Stripping and Refinishing

- Stain and dye application

- Restoring furniture

- Water-based and oil-based finishes

- An easy to understand approach to the subject theme

- The beginners guide on polishing, spraying, sanding, etc

- Fixing mistakes

- Troubleshooting

Written with you in mind to help solve your wood finishing fears as a beginner or an experienced hand needing a bit of refresher, this is a must-get book.

CLICK on the BUY button to begin finishing your wood with style today.

https://www.amazon.com/dp/B08LPJ6C9Z

Leather Crafting Beginner's Manual: A Step-by-Step Illustrated Guide with Basic Leatherworking Projects and Techniques

Explore the fantastic world of leather crafting that will give you joy for ages!

• Need to have manual for both beginners and experienced hands working with leather

• Detailed and well-explained facts about leather, tools, techniques, and projects to help you with leather crafting

• Become acquainted with the necessary methods through well-taught guides on the use of essential tools, leather preparation, and finishing.

• Understand and put to practice skills such as stitching, forming, braiding, molding, lacing and embossing

• Sequential photographic illustration of the different processes and tools

• Incredibly easy to craft projects for you!

Leather crafting is a timeless art that is not limited to any age bracket or skill level. If you are a pro in search of a brush-up material or a beginner needing proper grounding, Leather Crafting for Beginner's is your go-to manual for a fun crafting experience.

Clayton M. Rines introduce you to the foundations of leather, its structure, types, preparation, how to use embossing tools, awls, cutters, stamps, etc. He gives essential hints on how to braid, stitch and craft primary, intermediary, and difficult leatherworks.

This book contains;

- Historical facts about leather

- Cutting and making patterns

- Stitching

- Stamping

- Gluing

- Embossing

- Beveling

- Coloring

- Finishing

- How to care and source for leather

- Projects

- And so much more!

No matter the skill, project, or ideas that you want to implement on your leather piece such as the making of a leather bracelet, cufflinks, pouches, passport cover, Leather Mason Jar Koozie, amazing scrap leather projects, etc., you will find all that in this book and much more!

Begin your leatherworking journey today with that can-do attitude.

CLICK the buy button now!

https://www.amazon.com/dp/B08KH3T1PS

About the Author

Clayton M. Rines is a techie who lives in and around gadgets. Knowing what makes devices all around us tick is his life ambition, and he is always on the lookout for new ideas to everyday technological problems. Bringing solutions to your gadget issues, giving opinions and tips on how to get the best out of your devices, and bringing to you excellent news gives him so much pleasure. He is a DIY expert, naturalist and animal lover.

Clayton is from Sacramento, California and enjoys globetrotting, savoring new experiences, enjoying new cultures.

Made in United States
Troutdale, OR
07/31/2023

11709897R00076